Catching
AIR

Tilbury House Publishers
12 Starr St.
Thomaston, Maine 04861
800–582–1899 • www.tilburyhouse.com

First edition: March 2017 • 10 9 8 7 6 5 4 3 2 1

Library of Congress Control Number: 2016959412

ISBN: 978-0-88448-496-7

Designed by Frame25 Productions

Printed in Shenzhen, China, by Shenzhen Caimei Printing Co., Ltd.,
through Four Colour Print Group, Louisville, KY

Photo Credits

Front cover, Scott Linstead; title page, Scott Linstead; p.4, Scott Linstead; p.5 top left, Lee Yiu Tung c/o Shutterstock.com; p.5 top right, Scott Linstead; p.5 bottom, Scott Linstead; p.6 top, Scott Linstead; p.6 bottom, Satoshi Kuribayashi, Nature Production / Minden Pictures; p.7, Scott Linstead; p.8, Neagone Fo / Shutterstock; p.9 top, Scott Linstead; p.9 bottom left, Cede Prudente Photography; p.9 bottom right, Thawats / Thinkstock; p.10 top, Illustration by Meyers Konversations-Lexikon (1897) / Hein Nouwens / Shutterstock; p.10 bottom, Alfred Russel Wallace illustration from The Malay Archipelago / Wikimedia Commons; p.11, Ondrej Prosicky / Shutterstock; p.12 photo, Tony Campbell / Shutterstock; p.12 map, IUCN (International Union for the Conservation of Nature) Red List spatial data / Wikimedia Commons; p.13 top photo, P. J. Turgeon / Wikimedia Commons; p.13 central photo, Stephen Dalton / Minden Pictures; p.13 map, IUCN (International Union for the Conservation of Nature) Red List spatial data / Wikimedia Commons; p.14, blickwinkel / Alamy Stock Photo; p.15 top, Nineteenth-century illustration / Alamy Stock Photo; p.16, Dave M. Hunt Photography / Shutterstock; p.17, Scott Linstead; pp.18 – 19, Stephan Bidouze / Shutterstock; p.19 bottom, Felix Lipov / Shutterstock; p.20 – 21, Piyaphong / Shutterstock; p. 22, Vincent St. Thomas / Shutterstock; p.23 inset, Wikimedia Commons; p.23 central, Cede Prudente Photography; p.24: Ch'ien Lee / Minden Pictures; p.25, Stephen Dalton / Minden Pictures; p.26: reptiles4all / Thinkstock; p.27 top, Cede Prudente Photography; p.27 bottom, Alan Couch / Wikimedia Commons; p.28: Christian Ziegler / Minden Pictures; p.29 top, Prashanthns / Wikimedia Commons; p.29 bottom, St. George Jackson Mivart illustration, 1874 / Wikimedia Commons; p.30, Arthur Weasley / Wikimedia Commons; p.31, Pierre Lobel, Biosphoto / Minden Pictures; p.32 top, Dinostar Company, Ltd.; p.32 middle, Linda Bucklin / Shutterstock; p.32 bottom, Herschel Hoffmeyer / Shutterstock; p.33, Ivan Kuzmin / Shutterstock; p.34 top, Leo Blanchette / Shutterstock; p.34 bottom, Celso Diniz / Thinkstock; p.35, Sindre Espejord / Thinkstock; pp. 36 – 37, Iakov Kalinin / Shutterstock

Catching
AIR

Taking the Leap with Gliding Animals

SNEED B. COLLARD III

TILBURY HOUSE
PUBLISHERS

HIGH IN A PINE TREE in Southeast Asia,
A Draco lizard searches for ants to eat.
As it swivels its head, it stops . . .

4

. . . and stares into the eyes
of a deadly paradise tree snake.
The snake lunges!
The Draco leaps out into space.
With the ground a
hundred feet below,
death seems certain.

But the lizard doesn't fall.
Instead, it does something
almost no other animal
in the world can do.
It spreads its ribs and...

5

. . . IT GLIDES!

Like a fighter pilot,
the Draco zips around one
tree, pulls a sharp turn,
and makes a perfect landing
on the bark of another.

It blinks once. Twice.
Then, it scampers
up the tree trunk,
alive for another day.

THE DRACO LIZARD
belongs to one of earth's most
remarkable groups of animals.
Scientists call them gliders.
What do they do?

Well, gliding is not flying.
It is not falling, either.
It is something in between.

GLIDING OR PARACHUTING?

Many frogs and other tree-dwelling animals spread out their bodies to slow their falls from tall trees. Scientists call this *parachuting*. Parachuting, though, is not gliding. What's the difference? Scientists define parachuting animals as those that descend, or fall, toward earth at angles greater than 45 degrees—in other words, close to straight down. Gliders, on the other hand, descend toward earth at much shallower, or gentler, angles. As a result, gliders can travel great distances and control their directions as they descend. They can also make softer landings!

The smooth-backed gliding gecko is camouflaged to disappear on tree bark.

Many kinds of animals around the world have developed the ability to glide.
All gliders live in forests, where they find endless launch pads high above the ground.
Gliding saves these animals time as they move from tree to tree.

If they fall out of a tree by accident, gliding keeps them from getting injured.
Gliding can even keep them from becoming lunch for a predator.

Wallace's flying frog.

The red giant flying squirrel of Southeast Asia weighs up to six pounds— enormous for a gliding animal.

The colugo, or flying lemur.

HOW NATURE WORKS

DOES GLIDING SAVE ENERGY?

One thing gliding may *not* do for animals is save them energy. Several scientists attached a recording device to an animal called a colugo to figure out how much time and energy it spent gliding, climbing, and doing other activities. They discovered that large gliders use just as much energy gliding as they do walking or running. Why? Because these animals must *climb* before they can glide, and that burns a lot of calories.

9

Like the Draco lizard, most gliders spread special flaps on their bodies.

These flaps are called *patagia* (puh-TAY-jee-uh). A single flap is a patagium.

Patagia act like wings, or airfoils. With their patagia, gliders descend toward earth, but not too fast.

They ride the air across large distances and even control where they are going.

Wallace's flying frog drawn by Alfred Russel Wallace with its feet patagia spread.

PATAGIUM

PATAGIUM

The Philippine "flying lemur," or colugo, showing the patagia, or membranes, that connect its front and hind legs and tail.

A bird's wing has a curved upper surface and a flatter lower surface. This shape creates *lift* that pushes the bird upward, especially when it is flapping. Gliding animals are not capable of flapping flight.

Nevertheless, the patagia of many gliders—Draco lizards and flying squirrels, for instance—have a shape that is similar to a bird's wing.

Other patagia, such as those between the toes of flying frogs, are simpler folds of skin.

Once air is moving over a glider's body, all patagia can generate lift. This lift keeps the animals from falling straight down.

PATAGIA CAN BE ANYWHERE

Patagia can be located in many different parts of a glider's body: along the neck, at the base of the tail, between the toes—even, as in a Draco lizard, between the animal's ribs. Patagia are almost always made of loose skin, and can be covered by fur or scales. While walking or at rest, the patagia of most gliders are folded up and almost unnoticeable. Only when the animal leaps to glide does it spread its "wings."

A Southern flying squirrel by day, showing the big eyes of a nocturnal mammal.

Range of the Southern flying squirrel.

ALMOST 50 SPECIES of flying squirrels live in Asia, but only two species inhabit North America.

Both are *nocturnal*, active at night.

Both are also *omnivores*, feeding on nuts,

The Northern flying squirrel at rest and in the air.

For flying squirrels, the main advantage of gliding is probably to escape predators.

Owls, snakes, and larger mammals all hunt flying squirrels, but when they're in danger, the animals can glide up to 150 feet (45 meters) to reach safety.

Range of the Northern flying squirrel.

Want to see a flying squirrel for yourself? Try shining a light on a bird feeder at night.

African forests have their *anomalures* (a-no-mah-LOORZ), which are known as the scaly-tailed squirrels. At least seven species live in West Africa and the Congo.

These little-known rodents look like squirrels but are only distant cousins. During the day, dozens of anomalures may roost together in hollow trees.

At night, they travel miles in search of fruit, bark, leaves, flowers, and insects to eat.

A Lord Derby's anomalure in the Central African Republic.

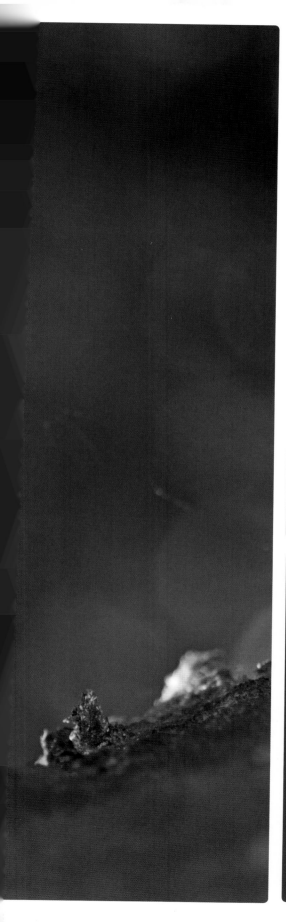

ANOMALURE FEATURES

Two rows of scales stick up from the base of an anomalure's tail. Scientists believe these scales help prevent the animals from slipping while they are clinging to tree trunks. Sticking out from an anomalure's front elbows are special "spreaders" made from cartilage. When  gliding, these help spread the large main patagium between the animal's front and back legs. Smaller patagia connect an anomalure's legs to its neck and tail.

15

For cuteness, it's hard
to beat Australia's
sugar gliders, shooting
between eucalyptus trees.

16

Most live in family groups and call loudly to each other as they glide through the tall forests where they live.

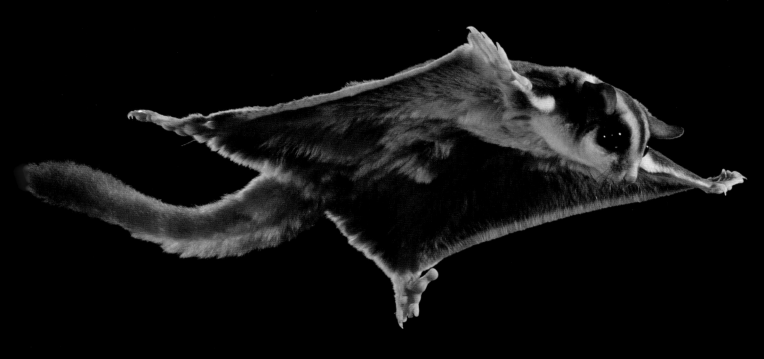

But to find the world's greatest collection of gliders, you must search the rainforests of...

SUGAR GLIDERS

Sugar gliders are one of at least eight species of gliding possums that live in Australia and the islands of Papua New Guinea. These nocturnal creatures feed on sap, flowers, insects, and other invertebrates. Although these gliders behave and look a lot like anomalures and flying squirrels, gliding possums are *marsupial mammals*. Their babies spend only a short time in the womb. Born before they are fully formed, they crawl into a pouch or pocket, where they feed on milk and continue to grow.

. . . SOUTHEAST ASIA.

Here, you will find more than fifty species of gliding lizards, five species of gliding snakes, thirty species of gliding squirrels, and an unknown number of gliding frogs. Why do more gliders live in Southeast Asia than anywhere else? Scientists have several ideas, or *theories*, about that.

One is that Southeast Asia's very tall trees make especially good launch pads for gliders.

The problem with this theory is that other forests have trees that grow just as tall, but don't have nearly as many gliders. Another theory is that Southeast Asian forests don't have many vines for animals to walk or crawl on to reach nearby trees. But again, other forests also lack vines, and very few gliders live in those other forests. So what is the true reason gliding has evolved so many times in Asian animals? Scientists have another idea . . .

Range of the Southeast Asian rainforest (shown in green).

REDWOODS

California redwoods are the planet's tallest trees, yet only one species of glider—the Northern flying squirrel—lives there. Australian eucalyptus trees also grow extremely tall, but are home to only a few species of gliding possums—and those don't live in Australia's tallest trees.

Southeast Asian forests are filled with plants called *dipterocarps* (DIP-ter-o-karps).

Many grow very tall.

Dipterocarp leaves, though, are loaded with toxins that make them difficult to digest.

Many dipterocarps also only flower and fruit every few years.

That means that fewer insects and other small prey animals can survive in these forests. When food is available, it is often separated by large distances.

Many scientists believe that in Southeast Asia, gliding evolved mainly as a fast way to move between food sources that are very far apart.

If that's true, gliding has succeeded wildly!

RAINFOREST TREES

Hundreds of species of dipterocarp trees fill the forests of Southeast Asia. Many flower and fruit all at the same time. By doing so, they overwhelm animals that eat their fruits and seeds. That improves the chances that some of the seeds will survive and sprout into new trees. Because most of the trees don't fruit every year, however, it means that in most years, animals have to work harder to find food.

21

MEET THE COLUGO, a relative of us primates. It can glide more than 400 feet (120 meters) to reach some tasty leaves to eat.

A colugo in the forests of Indonesia.

A female colugo gliding while a baby clings to her belly.

"FLYING LEMURS"

HOW NATURE WORKS

Colugos are often called "flying lemurs"—even though they bear no relation to the famous lemurs of Madagascar. Shy, nocturnal mammals, colugus can weigh more than four pounds. That makes them some of the world's heaviest gliders. Fortunately, colugos have supersized patagia that carry them exceptional distances. They also have long digestive tracts that help them digest a wide variety of leaves, flowers, and other vegetation. Even though they are superb gliders, colugos are clumsy climbers. They have to kind of scoot and hop up a tree trunk. It's a good thing they only have to climb once in a while!

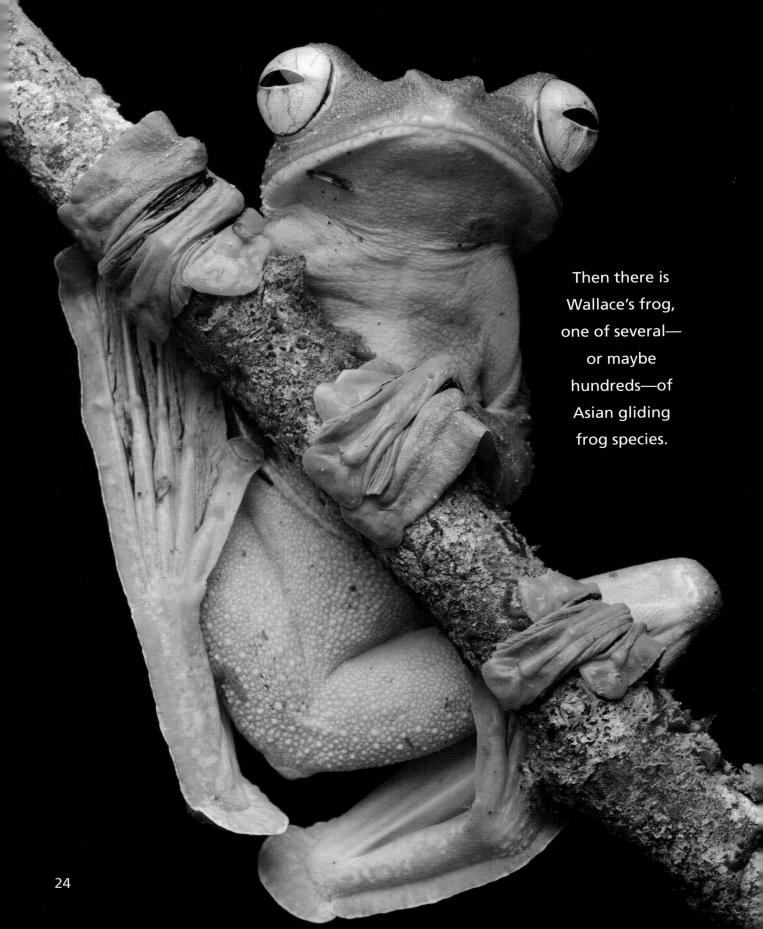

Then there is
Wallace's frog,
one of several—
or maybe
hundreds—of
Asian gliding
frog species.

24

FLYING FROGS

Southeast Asia's famous "flying frogs" belong to the genus *Rhacophorus*. Scientists consider them the weakest gliders, but these frogs still can sail large distances and even change direction in midflight. They spend most of their lives up in trees chasing and eating insects, but swoop down to pools of water to mate and lay eggs. No one is sure how many gliding frogs exist. Scientists know of several gliding species, but haven't studied most of the 380 or so species of *Rhacophorus* to see if they also can glide. It is fitting that the most famous gliding frog, Wallace's frog, is named after Alfred Russel Wallace—the man who, along with Charles Darwin, came up with the modern theory of evolution.

Perhaps the most startling of all gliding animals are five species of gliding snakes.

Above and opposite: Paradise tree snakes in Borneo.

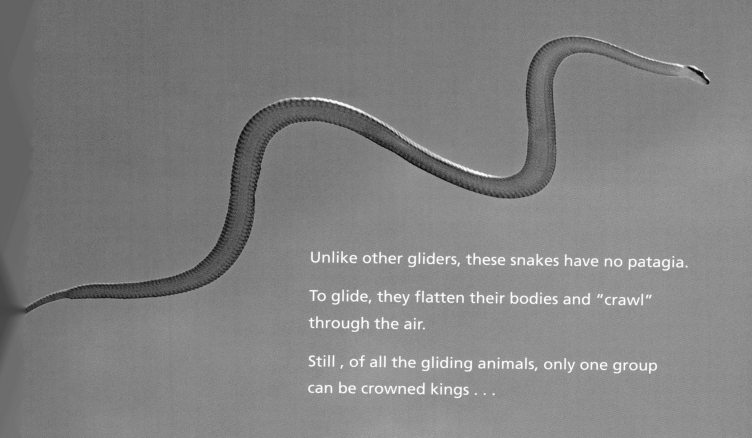

Unlike other gliders, these snakes have no patagia.

To glide, they flatten their bodies and "crawl" through the air.

Still , of all the gliding animals, only one group can be crowned kings . . .

AND SNAKES TOO?

All five species of gliding snakes—including the paradise tree snake—belong to the genus *Chrysopelea*. These snakes grow only to about three feet (one meter) long, and often prey on Draco lizards. For these snakes, gliding may have evolved as an advantage to chasing their lizard prey. When they glide, the snakes flatten and curve their bodies. They appear to crawl or swim through the air. Scientists aren't sure how these crawling movements help the snakes glide, but they seem to work. The snakes can travel more than 100 feet (30 meters) from their takeoff points and make fast, precise turns in mid-flight.

. . . THE DRACO LIZARDS.

Spreading their ribs out into large "fans," these lizards fly circles around most other gliders.

They use their amazing skills to locate food, chase off competing Draco lizards, and even impress their mates.

A Draco lizard in Malaysia.

A Draco lizard in South India showing its camouflage.

THE WORLD'S BEST GLIDERS

HOW NATURE WORKS

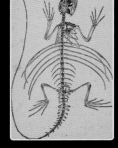

Draco lizards are the only gliders with patagia supported by bones—in this case, their ribs. Muscles control how far the patagia extend, or spread out. This gives the lizards an amazing ability to control their glides. Dracos have an additional set of patagia under their chins. These *lappets* provide the animals with extra lift and control. Even the legs of Draco lizards are shaped like airfoils! Dracos spend almost their entire lives in the trees. Only the females come to the ground, to lay eggs. Males stake out territories in their treetop homes. Besides helping him glide, a male's colorful patagia attract mates and warn other males to stay out of his "no-fly zone." Smaller Draco species outglide bigger ones. Why? Because larger Dracos have greater *wing loading*. That means that the same area of the patagia must lift a greater weight than in smaller lizards.

BUT DRACO LIZARDS and today's other gliders are not the first animals to glide!

Starting about 125 million years ago, some early mammals evolved the ability to glide.

Before that, so did a few fish.

GLIDING ISN'T NEW

Fossils prove that gliding evolved several times in ancient mammals. The earliest known mammalian glider, *Volaticotherium antiquus*, lived at least 125 million years ago. It had a large patagium covered with thick fur. The next known gliding mammal was a small rodent that lived about 30 million years ago. Why weren't there any gliding mammals between those two time periods? There probably were. Only a few animal remains ever turn into fossils, however, so we may never find evidence for these missing mammals.

Volaticotherium antiquus.

Flying fish at Cocos Island, Costa Rica.

FLYING FISH

HOW NATURE
WORKS

Both ancient and modern fishes have evolved the ability to glide. For fishes, gliding developed mostly as a means to escape predators. The earliest fossil of a gliding fish—240 million years old—comes from China. The fish had long pectoral fins that could serve as wings. It also had a forked tail with a very large bottom lobe. By rapidly swishing its tail back and forth, the fish could generate enough speed to launch it into the air and over the water surface. Today's 64 or so species of "flying fishes" are not related to this ancient fossil but have evolved similar gliding equipment.

Many dinosaurs glided. Some paved the way for flying birds.

Which brings up an interesting question...

Yi Qi, the Chinese gliding dinosaur.

THE EVOLUTION OF BIRDS

Scientists believe that modern birds descended from gliding dinosaurs. Anchiornis lived about 155 million years ago. Archaeopteryx lived about 152 million years ago. Both species had limbs covered in feathers, and almost definitely could glide. Gliding probably helped these animals find food and escape predators—just as it does for gliders today. Neither of these dinosaurs could actually fly, but scientists believe they were important stepping stones in the evolution of modern flying birds.

Archaeopteryx

Will today's Draco lizards or other gliding animals ever evolve the ability to fly? That's not an easy question to answer.

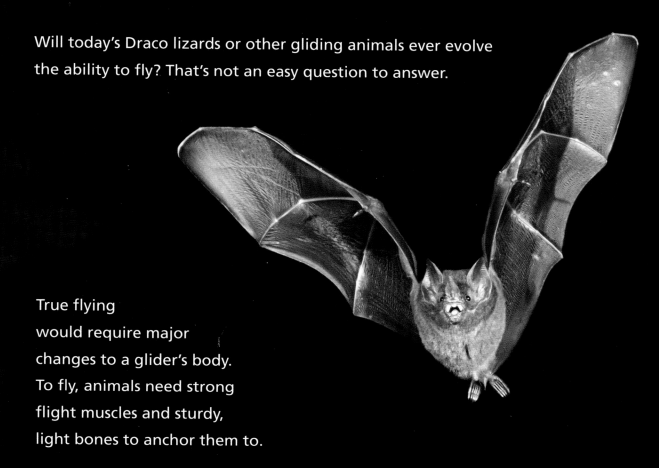

True flying would require major changes to a glider's body. To fly, animals need strong flight muscles and sturdy, light bones to anchor them to.

Then again, in the history of life on earth, stranger things have happened. Meanwhile, the world does have some astonishing new gliding animals . . .

GLIDING ISN'T FLYING

Scientists believe that both birds and bats evolved from gliding ancestors. That doesn't mean it was easy! Flapping flight requires extremely strong muscles to move the wings—along with bones to attach them to. It's hard to imagine that the patagia, muscles, and skeletons of a Draco lizard or a gliding frog could ever evolve into useful flapping wings. Just as important, true flight might not benefit today's gliding animals. If a new ability or feature does not improve the survival of a species, that feature usually will disappear—or never evolve in the first place. If any of today's gliding animals ever *do* evolve to fly, scientists bet that it might be a mammal such as a colugo or flying squirrel. These animals probably have skeletons and muscles that, over time, *could* evolve a true flying capability. True flight might also give them a better chance to survive.

. . . PEOPLE!

For many decades, people have tested the skies with gliding planes and hang gliders.

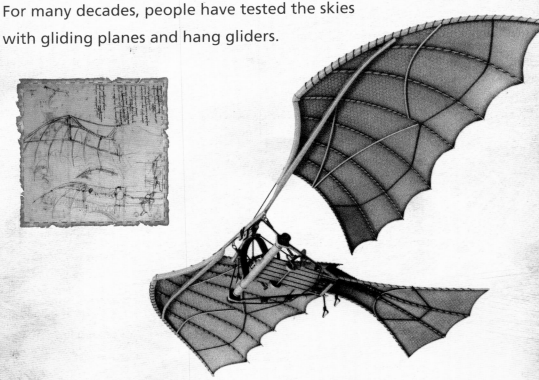

Leonardo da Vinci's ornithopter design from the late fifteenth century.

HANG GLIDERS

Manned glider flights took place at least as far back as 1,140 years ago. Early gliding machines were very primitive. Many crashed. However, by the time World War II rolled around, fleets of gliders that looked like motorless airplanes could deliver thousands of paratroopers behind enemy lines. Since the early 1960s, people have been building and improving modern hang gliders that can be flown by a single person. Some of today's high-performance hang gliders have glide ratios of up to 19:1. That means that in still air, they can travel 19 feet or meters forward for every foot or meter they drop toward earth. When pilots can find and catch rising columns of warm air called *thermals*, they can fly for hours. In 2012, two hang glider pilots set the world distance record for hang gliding by traveling more than 470 miles (750 km)—almost completely across the state of Texas!

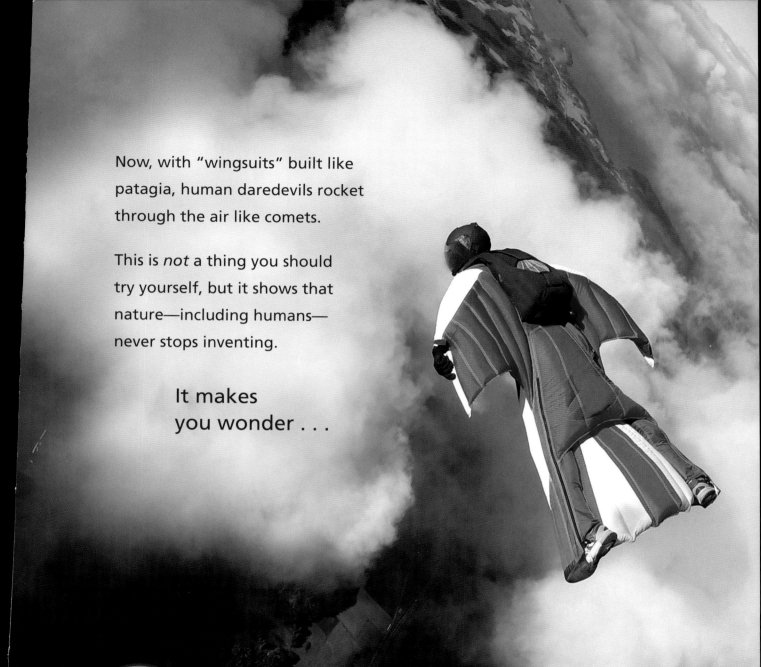

Now, with "wingsuits" built like patagia, human daredevils rocket through the air like comets.

This is *not* a thing you should try yourself, but it shows that nature—including humans—never stops inventing.

It makes
you wonder . . .

WINGSUITS

In the 1990s, inventors developed the first successful wingsuits. These closely mimic the patagia in gliding mammals. Most wingsuit flyers jump out of airplanes. After gliding for a while, they pull parachutes and float to the ground. BASE jumpers also wear parachutes, but leap from tall cliffs and mountains. This is an extremely dangerous activity, and many of the best BASE jumpers are killed in gliding accidents. NOTE: *Gliders and wingsuits are built by professional engineers. Do not ever try to build your own wingsuit or hang glider. You are very likely to get killed or injured.*

What will nature invent next?

Learning More About Gliders

When it comes to gliding animals, surprisingly little has been written—and almost nothing for young people. Several children's books mention gliders, including Natalie Lunis's *Gravity-Defying Animals (Animals with Super Powers)* (Bearport Publishing 2014). Several other books specifically focus on flying squirrels and sugar gliders because people keep these animals as pets—an activity I do *not* encourage.

Probably the best ways to learn about gliders is to check out expert websites on gliders, and watch some of the amazing videos of gliding animals available on YouTube. I have listed a few of my favorite links below, along with a few adult books for those who are especially passionate about these remarkable critters!

Online Websites

UC Berkeley's Museum of Paleontology's website on flight: *http://www.ucmp.berkeley.edu/vertebrates/flight/enter.html*

The University of Cambridge's Map of Life page on gliders and the evolution of flight: *http://www.mapoflife.org/topics/topic_342_Gliding-reptiles/*

"Borneo's Wild Gliders" by Tim Laman, an article published by the National Wildlife Federation. Link: *http://www.nwf.org/news-and-magazines/national-wildlife/animals/archives/2008/borneos-wild-gliders.aspx*

"Meet the Scaly-Tail Gliders" by Darren Naish, an outstanding blog article written by an eminent paleontologist from England. *http://blogs.scientificamerican.com/tetrapod-zoology/meet-the-scaly-tail-gliders/*

Also check out Darren Naish's article "There's so much more to flying frogs than flying frogs" at *http://blogs.scientificamerican.com/tetrapod-zoology/there-is-so-much-more-to-flying-frogs-than-flying/*

To find mind-boggling YouTube videos showing gliding animals, run searches on "gliding snakes", "flying frogs", "Draco lizards", and other gliding species.

Adult Books

Corlett, Richard T. and Richard B. Primack. *Tropical Rain Forests: An Ecological and Biogeographical Comparison* (2nd edition).Wiley-Blackwell, Oxford, 2011.

Jackson, Stephen. *Gliding Mammals of the World.* CSIRO Publishing, Clayton, 2012.

Pickrell, John. *Flying Dinosaurs: How Fearsome Reptiles Became Birds.* Columbia University Press, New York, 2014.

Gliding Words and Phrases

adapt: to change in a way that helps an animal survive changing circumstances

airfoil: a wing or other structure with curved surfaces that create lift

cartilage: firm tissue that is softer than bone, but still provides support for an animal's body parts

dipterocarp: a plant that belongs to a large family of tropical plants that all have fruits with two lobes or "wings"

evolve: to change; in living things, this happens through two processes, mutation and natural selection

flight: the ability to rise above the forces of gravity and move freely through the atmosphere or space

fossil: an organism or trace of a living thing, such as a footprint, that has been preserved through one of several different geological or other processes

genus: the name for a group of very closely related living things; it is part of the system for how scientists name and classify all life on earth

glide ratio: the distance something moves through air horizontally compared to how much it falls, or descends, due to gravity

lappet: a fold of skin that can be extended from the throat area of a Draco lizard and some other animals

lift: a force or forces that raise an object or animal higher, countering the force of gravity

marsupials, or **marsupial mammals:** kangaroos, wombats, possums, and similar animals in which young develop partly outside the womb, in special pouches

nocturnal: an organism that is active mostly at night

omnivore: an animal that eats a wide variety of plant and animal food

parachuting: spreading out one's body to increase the air resistance during a fall, thereby slowing the speed of the fall

patagium (plural: patagia): a fold or flap of skin that can be extended into an airfoil that helps increase an animal's glide ratio

theory: an idea that may help explain something that we don't understand; scientists often test theories to help determine if they are true

thermals: rising columns of warm air created by the sun's heating of the earth

wing loading: the amount of weight that a fixed area of a wing or airfoil must support

SNEED B. COLLARD III has glided through more than 80 books on his way to becoming one of today's best-known science writers for young people. After graduating with honors in marine biology from U.C. Berkeley, he went on to earn a master's degree in scientific instrumentation. Since then, he has traveled the world to research and photograph his award-winning science books. To learn more about Sneed and his books, or learn about his author visits and workshops, visit his website, www.sneedbcollardiii.com.

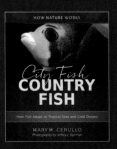
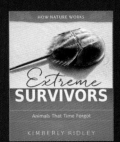